it was today

new poems
by andrei codrescu

For Toma

Andrei Codrescu

June 19 2004

Bellingham

COFFEE HOUSE PRESS

MINNEAPOLIS

Coffee House Press books are available to the trade through our primary distributor, Consortium Book Sales & Distribution, 1045 Westgate Drive, Saint Paul, MN 55114. For personal orders, catalogs, or other information, write to: Coffee House Press, 27 North Fourth Street, Suite 400, Minneapolis, MN 55401.

Coffee House Press is a nonprofit literary publishing house. Support from private foundations, corporate giving programs, government programs, and generous individuals help make the publication of our books possible. We gratefully acknowledge their support in detail in the back of this book.

LIBRARY OF CONGRESS CIP INFORMATION

Codrescu, Andrei
it was today : new poems / by Andrei Codrescu. — 1st ed.
p. cm.
ISBN 1-56689-146-9 (alk. paper) paperback
ISBN 1-56689-150-7 (alk. paper) cloth
I. Title.

PS3553.03185 2003
811'.54—DC21
2003055097

1 3 5 7 9 8 6 4 2

FIRST PRINTING | FIRST EDITION

PRINTED IN THE UNITED STATES

Good books are brewing at coffeehousepress.org

contents

1.

2. LU LI & WENG LI

3.

one

the fire truck comes to your house

full of smoke
you get to scoop smoke into jars
with a spoon
as much as you want
I know I'm the fire chief
a week from now
I'll order the sirens
out of the oceans
and into the streets
to inform you about smoke
my men have big mustaches
the sirens'll do anything
we ask them to do even sing

we live

among so many ends
terminals
finals
it's a wonder we don't end
every minute
the miracle is that we continue
among the detritus of the ends
of others
to carry on
fueled by curiosity
tattered passion
all sorts of small patched engines
the seas are rough yes
our craft leaks
but we will gain rhodes yet

once

once more young minds
take to the rough via
of self-consciousness
paved with mastodons'
lumbering thoughts of
getting home in more
comfortable bodies
once more the shadows flee
the advent of electricity
it will be up to you
to either bemoan
what lived outside
the halos of candles
or get on with what you see
there the thing ungainly
oh love oh road companion
once more we set sail
for the age of awkwardness
we started from
until they invent
the everyday x ray
there are still plenty
of things that aren't there
sweetened only by horniness
oh phantom
a sultan built you for sex

a nantucket sleigh ride

where language is snow
stories are walls
& thor and buddha talk
& the talibanists eat
the past like a salted
serpent from the guts
of darkness surrounding
the tiny lit island
of civilized congress—
gotta make the island bigger!

houses, scams, language

(with a line in romanian)

silver & gossamer & porcelain & cobwebs
some people are made out of
they walk from here to there
a limited number of times only—
but the bony phone is just dumb plastic
it rings not at all

i don't understand: my ideas are universal
but my audience is five guys at the shell
station people just don't get it

she longs for what makes her grin
(tînjește după ce rînjește)
the sweetness of want
the repulsiveness of having
after days she was returned
by the storms of language
that had tossed her far
& she rearranged her face
for the english language—

what i heard i did not hear
what i saw i did not see
i trust my sense to dullness then
i kill my joy & cease to be

nickelodeon

have 20th century
hangover in change
jars good american
change while paper
in denominations
of one million per
square toilet roll
fills the empty
dreams of romanians
with numbers not much
else certainly not
sausages on a grill
with new wine in love
in let's say 1965
when nothing not even
communism could stop
the sap from overcoming
the ballyhooed and now
forgotten curtain
I had a youth once
I was very good at it

1968 for leonard cohen

the party was on the roof
of the chelsea hotel
above shelley winters' penthouse
a summer breeze started up
new york came to life in the evening
the girls began taking off their shirts
to dance
I was in heaven
I felt so glamorous
I was nineteen years old
and so was the world
I was but a year out of the old world
the ancient murderous world
dressed in black from head to foot
still mourning sorrows I was beginning
to forget
the night was rose and soft
the girls were dancing bare-breasted
ah, what better place to be
a young poet in the late century
dancing with a sleepy-eyed beauty
with foam still clinging to her sea-fresh body
I closed my eyes

when I opened them
all the girls had vanished
I panicked
had the barbarians come
made off with the women?

no said someone
it was rumored that bob dylan
was visiting leonard cohen
in his room
and all the girls went there

the barbarians
were our heroes

january 3 2001

awesomeness of numbers
fooled me my whole life
their significance it turns
out turns you out no matter
how familiar they manage
to look they are not they
are the agents of time we
invented them to banish
amorphous chaos not
realizing that in that chaos
lay the rich amorphs
of eternity and gushy
edenstuff & now numbers
we got & they tantalize us
with their near-nakedness

we diced the cabbage
I wanted to say & stared
down the one-eyed peas
the black-eyed good-luck
peas and money-holding
cabbage of local new year
custom & the trouble was
last year that I allowed
holey cabbage to suck
away my money not this
year sir no not this year

this is the year of poesy
and cash no more mr. nice
guy attila the hun is here

he yields the paradox blade
on your knees agents
of mishmeal mediocrities
celeric crap peddlers & all
bores of every stripe go
down on your knees empty
your pockets & sing to me
that song OK that goes we
are singing to you and paying
you to look how much a lot

to poetry

that nervous energy
is called poetry
when you can't stand
either still or the world
it's that groove
even half asleep
because the pharmacy
of control the chemical
frame around the window
of liberty is stealing
away half the energy
even then the nervous
half-asleep energy
is still poetry
in full bloom
the window open
you crawl through
to get to the bar
and to the girls
is really open to poetry
so this year go there

haiku + one

bad weather all over europe
strange dreams
fascists win in russia

poetry is foremost the desire for poetry

birthday poem & bed-frame I.O.U.

for my love 9/27/01

and for your birthday
what should I get you
1.7 acres with a pond
shoes with jewels or
pampering at the spa?
eggs in bed, you said
I want you to make me
eggs the way you make
them fluffy scrambled—
so you get up before me
and make me coffee
instead and I don't get
to make you eggs in bed
and the war is on TV
and it's yom kippur
I know that what you
really want is a bed frame
to turn the bed into a ship
a book-ship to read in
as we set sail through
the rocky century ahead
hold steady, baby
magellan loves you

the portuguese eat a dish

called feijoada
heavy with beans
cabbages potatoes ham
kale roasted manioc
orange slices on top
the jews eat a similar
dish sans ham
called cholent
they took it with them
to brazil every saturday
on one side of the street
the jews eat their beans
while on the other
the maranos eat theirs
brazil said the poet machado
is sometimes a hambone

laura

is hungover
like a petrarchan sonnet

she went to bed smoking
after a night of debauchery
only fragments of which survive

in the telling

she ate the scrambled eggs
she didn't think she ordered
tried to drive the car
she forgot to bring

she's a wild-haired mess

somebody's reading her notes
she left them at the bar last night
along with all the boys
who wanted her

or so she says

she's work
is what I say

after twenty-five years

of typing with one finger
twenty-five published books
forty unpublished ones

my finger is giving out

my wrist hurts
it's not the typing
it's the clitoris
and all the masturbating

and the pointing

an impolite finger
j'accuse no more

old snake ponders

Heavens! What symptoms are these? Unrelenting
Synchronicity followed by sheer idiocy why me?
The serpent swallows his tail or is about to and is
Amazed to find how much older his tail has gotten
But even as he swallows he is not without hope of
Finding his old tail the delyumicious young tail
He used to chew on for hours when he was bored
In class This just can't be the same tail so maybe
He shouldn't swallow it even though he's in a
Swallowing tail kind of mood and he knows only
Too well that there is no more snake afterwards
So this must be a cosmic joke set up by his dead
Friends either that or this kind of thing in subtler
Forms goes on all the time and snakes everywhere
Disappear routinely under the pressure
Of synchronicity What makes him such a special snake?
And the sheer idiocy is there to exhaust him
Long enough to consider such matters O snake
You are long silly belt-like greedy and stupid!

my name is andrei codrescu

My first book of poetry was called *License to Carry a Gun.*
It was written in 1968.
1968 was the year when guns took down
Martin Luther King and Robert Kennedy.
The title of my book meant that in a crazy time
one had to be crazier
and that meant not just having a gun
but BEING a gun.
Later that year at a poetry reading
a group of us "shot" some boring poets
with fake guns while shouting
"Death to Bourgeois Poetry!"
and after the poetry reading
I was busted by two plainclothes policemen
who said I had just robbed a store
with my fake gun
and later that year
I got held up at gunpoint.
And later yet
in August of 1996
Jonathan Ferrara handed me a twisted machine-pistol
at a poetry reading
(there were only a few boring bourgeois poets there)
and told me to make art out of it
and I gave the gun to my son to hold
without telling him that I was supposed to make
art out of it
and he put it in his backpack

and later yet
he dropped it in a garbage can
on his way home.
This is why there is no gun here
only a poem.
And when I said to my son: shit,
what am I gonna do with no gun?
he said: You made enough art
out of guns already.
Let this one pass.

my son came over

my son and I
said I didn't
want to see no
thracian charm
bracelets to read
the mysterious
inscriptions on them
though the dacians
were the ancestors
of romanians and I
might have by some
metempsychotic
process deciphered
them and no I said
I didn't want
to paddle for an hour
on the lake in city
park but I might
want to take up
a sport sometime
and we went through
all the sports I
might take up and I
decided against tennis
handball racquetball
or running because they
kill guys my age
just this year my friend
tom dent died playing
tennis and maybe I

wanted to swim and my son
said that you can play
all sports relaxed and I
said let's play chess
and when we came
to my place I said
not today maybe some
other time I
am a horrid and cranky
old man but my son
said sweetly some other
time so tomorrow
we will translate poems
from the spanish they
are about how hard
the world is and I
think that they are also
about mean old men but I
hope that they are about joy

greetings they weren't using then

I walked past jeremy in the park
whassup, j? I said having last
seen him on castro street ca. 1976
following some guy 'too busy to
talk right now I'm following some guy
I had sex all night it wasn't enough.'
this time he was imaginary
'reaching cruising altitude,' he said,
cruising, he was always cruising,
cruised to venus according to jeff
who kept track of the disappeared
he joined them not long after
and that is a form:
the last time I saw so-and-so
form we are becoming all-too-adept
at practicing these days
all I wanted to say was chartreuse
about being alone or something
or cinnamon or how I met somebody
at ocher & main but jeremy showed up
whassup whassup whassup

as tears go by

I want to cry whenever I hear Marianne Faithfull sing "As Tears Go By" because she's watching children play and children always make me cry because I think that it's a big bad world that's mean to children. It was mean to me, certainly, when I was a child. I cried when my mother left me with my grandmother. I cried when my grandmother left me at school. I cried when my father left the country—and us—forever. I cried when Stalin died.

I cried when my mother cried. And that was often. Her tears were both specific and generic. They were specific when it was a matter of a man leaving her. They were generic when she cried because life and the world were unbearable. And sometimes she cried neither specifically nor generically but deeper like an animal. And those were not her tears, they were the tears of unfairness for being a woman, for being a Jew, for being punished for something she didn't know the name of. I sometimes cried with her like that and those tears just flowed through us on their way somewhere else: they were part of a river of tears that runs through our kind since the beginning of time. This river sweeps us all in its swell and we stand in it keening, wailing, and arguing with something invisible in the language of lamentations. My mother's two aunts, my grandmother's sisters, who died at Auschwitz, were swept away by this river.

I rarely cry now. Sometimes I'm filled by love or sorrow and I feel the tears rising—but I usually check them. I did cry when Romania overthrew the Ceaușescu dictatorship. Prematurely, perhaps. I'm afraid that if I start crying I'll never stop. Not for any particular, or even generic reason. But for that animal reason that leads to the river of tears.

In Romanian folk tales the tears of young girls become flowers. But what happens to the tears of aging poets? They become sharpened spikes, rusted bollards, fish hooks, spears, barbed wire. . . . Their tears are bitter! Keep the poets from crying!

draft

God saith
people are typos
no proofreader
on Sunday

a geography of poets

is all wrong, ed

what poets now live
where they say they do
where they started out
where they want to

half the midwesterners
did time in new york
the other half in california

only new yorkers write
as if they are from new york
and mostly they are not

the ones in california
were wounded elsewhere
when they feel better
or can't afford the rent
they'll go back where
they came from

this is america
you get hurt where you are born
you make poetry out of it
as far from home as you can get
you die somewhere in between

the only geography of poets
is greyhound
general motors rules them all
ubi patria ibi bene
or ibi bene ubi patria
bread out of nostalgia
not a lot of it either
some of us came from very far
maps don't help much

my sympathy

is with those
who see without
plainly their
selves properly
miniaturized
but my heart skips
a beat when one
of them takes off
leaving the facts
to themselves
only the flame visible
the deeper chords
touched insouciantly

defense of the meek

the meek have taken
jesus to mean
their turn will come
jesus was merely
stating a fact the meek
will inherit the earth
there are more of them
or he may have been mean
and a buddhist and meant
the meek will return
to the earth over
and over until they get
it right sometimes
translation is on the side
of the meek but never
the commentary

Poetry, the ancients said.

We are the ancients now.
Poetry, the ancients said,
must be true to the last drop.
When the body is cold is when
the poet knows his reader
has at last gotten it.
Poets? A bunch of murderers
if you want my opinion.
Being one of them doesn't
make it any better.
I make it any way I can.

to the museum curators

you can see them at parties
in power suits
surprisingly their ideas
were your ideas
when you were twenty-three
you went on to think them through
they kept them
their persons grew around them
a pulpy mass around half-baked seeds
now they won't let you talk
they flash their gold cards
drown you under the weight
they fear your seeing the plain flaw
you do plainly
no amount of gold flesh can hide it
maybe they weren't your children in the first place
it was all second hand
their shyness kept them from being what
they always were windbags charlatans frauds
they know it's only for a minute
only their worship of you and the bad habits
you have bestowed on them
keep them from being pure fertilizer
they are more laughable than tragic
but they do not serve the public good
everyone goes a little bad in their wake

to a young poet

so poetry
aha they go
I write it
I want to publish it
I am the new flock
I have been taught
in school by many
renowned poets
all of them great
mediocrities & now
I want to put my self-
consciousness to use
by you so you can
recommend me for prizes
grants fame & then maybe
you can call my mom
& say yes he made some-
thing of himself he's a poet
& then if you publish a big
book of poems I'll read
one or two & give you my
begrudging approval in the name
of the new flock even though
we are lost & nobody cares
if we live or we die & our
web sites go unlogged on
maybe they need more sex
the sex we are not having
much of because your fucking
generation had it all plus

egos to match & we hate you
even those two poems I didn't
quite finish from your big new
book books are dead don't
you know it

on drunkenness

I write my poems sober
I read them drunk
Unlike many poets
Before me who wrote
Them drunk read them drunk
And even stayed drunk
During other peoples'
Readings and in this
They succeeded admirably
They are mostly dead now
In poetry we call this success
After we die people read
Our poems to their sweethearts
And friends and it's a fair
Bet that they are drunk when
They do this god forbid
That they should begin
Writing their own
Drinking gets passed on
Poetry rarely
Baudelaire was right
Enivrêz-vous mais
Seulement au but d'être pissés
Pas pour la poèsie
That is to say drink if you must
But don't do it for poetry please
Things are bad enough as it is

young men write poetry

about being raped by girls
in my class
girls write about men
knowing nothing
nobody is happy
but the girl in front of me
has gone from shorts to a mini
next week the white panties
have to go
it is not the flesh they complain about
it is the lack of lust
the soul
which used to belong to everybody
is now being hoarded
by old men
thank god I have the key
to knowing this
next week
the panties will go
you read it here

I hate youth

in the morning
they are fresh
drinking all night
killed me
but look at them
fucking youth
they are still alive
if they keep looking
like that I'll kill
them myself
so write it down
when the profession
demands
but keep that youth away

the masses

they knew
what everyone knew
they said
what everyone said
they did
what their predecessors did
when there was war they died
in corn rows & were plowed under
when there wasn't
they ate too much & were bitter
they were remembered
vaguely by many people
well by one or two
politicians used them in speeches

taxes

is what you give in caesar's salad
to the accountant
who is coming
all the way from white america
to keep you honest
your salad days are over
you go for the jugular now
some vegetarian!

the dorkery

is full
even the trough groans
they get in your phone
they get in your hair
communication has made them ubiquitous
now they can spread vapidity and greed
they pick their noses in public
they puff huff spray dork-essence
cut their phone lines
smother their faxes
seize their means of communication
better even cut your own cord
how can they reach you when you live now
in the dark they just escaped from
let them have the light
if they let you have
just a little corner of the night

morning hike

chautauqua june 24 2002

if you meet a mountain lion
on the enchanted mesa path
look like Ted Berrigan big
say funny things flap your
arms and the lion will laugh
and go away or failing that
stand up and fight
it's different with bears
with them you roll yourself
in a ball and roll away down
the mountain more like let's
say e.e. cummings or Aesop

for lynn luria sukenick

in memoriam may 1996

What if there is no story
only a feeling?
Of course there are many stories
in that feeling
only they didn't happen to me
they either just happened
to someone else
or happened a long time ago
and so recent and ancient
the stories hung in that feeling
like clusters of grapes
refreshing and intelligent
& I had the honor to drink in
their presence on one or two occasions
in the sap-filled & haunted
days of the late nineteen sixties
in the haunted late city of Santa Cruz
in the soon-to-be haunted state
of California just waking up
in those days in the embrace
of Ronald Reagan future
President of Star Wars winner
of the Cold War
& in that sexy intelligence
of Lynn's there was both wisdom & escape
though there was no story
only a feeling
& in those days most feelings came
before there was a story
so we bumped into stories
just to have something to hold

all that feeling
there were many stories
but with Lynn & for Lynn
only a feeling

dream of january 11, 1999 after the first copies of *messi@h* arrived & laura & i celebrated at molly's and it was gwen albert's birthday too

the emir rode on horseback
scattering gold coins along the wadde
the dry riverbed
for many miles into the desert
& the people went looking for the gold coins
& they could carry away as many
as they could find
but the one to find the last coin
would be put to death
decapitated as tradition called for
& I walked the wadde toward the end
deep in the desert
& I found many gold coins
just lying there on top of cracked earth
some of them half-buried
& I filled my pockets with them
& the very last find was a whole
roll of large round gulden with black
borders around their gold middles
& I stuck these in my back pocket
& knew somehow that among these
was the last coin so I better
get the hell out of this emirate
out of the desert if I wanted
to keep my head & as I walked
up the old dry riverbed fast I was
weighed down by this armor of gold

43

& it bothered me that the last roll
was kind of sticking out of my back pocket
easy to spot & I thought about sewing it
inside my sheepskin jacket
& then I was walking through the desert
toward las vegas in the distance
& I knew that if I could get there
I would be safe & escape decapitation
for having found the last coin
in the emir's desert country
& I stopped at a bank and put most
of the coins in a vault wrapped in shiny
white paper but kept the last roll
& one way it occurred to me
to escape the cursed coin
—which doubtless had a tiny transmitter on it—
was to keep walking & moving
& having other people hold the coins
& move evenly in circles to confuse
my pursuers

I need a pony

that was a projection

my girlfriend
wants a baby
or a pony
but mostly a baby

I'm just a pony
does she want me?

sometimes

what am I? art?

sperm-glut?
on the plane?
next one home?

is it french
to ask question
(s)

is it child first
or are best lines
communal agape?

I am first baby
& honorary woman

& the way car windows
go up?
am I car?

Tsar
OK

new orleans aubade

wake-up call
from fierce anger
I want to kill
everyone
but then it's only
my oversensitized
soul calling
for grace
or a nicotine fit—
I want out of here—
the legless armless
child ferociously
fearlessly swinging
in the dark park
as the proteus head
goes past
big hulking ship
pulling the dead nymph-child
more bird or dolphin
than child
swings and swings
picks a strand of pearls
with a flipper
in midair
drapes them
around his neck—
he has an angel's head
a golden torso
he is an event
in a sea of metaphors
wind-borne meat comet

another year

the wheel of history creaks
as I go around tattooing strangers' breasts
with temporary snakes
at street party on magnolia
monitored by floodlights
of the police as the supreme
courts proliferate on TV
whose country is it anyway
and is the hangover worse
from one or the other?

when dreams get thick on easy street
for jeffrey miller

when dreams get thick on easy street
the phone calls multiply
ivan gets his marching orders from jeff
hungarians make movies of jeff
jeff's every friend is mobilized
photography and telecommunications
slough off the world's meat body
while real cannibals like dahmer
make a post-movie appearance
in configurations reminiscent
of jeff's fascination.
jeff must be getting translated up there.
he wants to be translated down here.
tenure up there depends entirely
on not being forgotten down here.
laura and I write a clothing dictionary.
reality and appearance continue
to be as relevant as mind and body.
alice paints rows of buddhists
watching our friends' circuses
while people real and unreal continue
feeling real and unreal pain
and now and then an urge to write
and smile. so what's busy
got to do with it. the real work
is a book of old dreams collected
by new ones powder-like for yeast

sleeping with an open eye

open to what
the world's under water
laura needs to give birth
to herself now that her long-
range emotional plan
of bringing father back
to the fold has succeeded
three days of rain & still leaden
while my own emotional
program that of overthrowing
or becoming the father
I made up is endless—
unless one's program is endless
one must have a backup plan
which is why one walks around
the LSU lakes in the early A.M.
and says hello to everyone
he meets though many of them
look worse than him—
how does one live?

opera later

wearing a flock of blackbirds around his head
pointing with a lit cigarette to joan of arc mounted
atop her horse in the french quarter in new orleans

is Midnight Man

there are a lot of masseuses

named christi
I know two of them
service with a loincloth
ah generous world

*

the geometry of failure

wide hips
round heels
stiff rod
eye twinkle
everywhere but here

*

the unread books
are mad at me

soaking in rich people's tubs

under the stars
all they want is to be kissed
and when life takes a detour
and they go slumming
the irritation is greater
than the adventure
peace and quiet more important
you could always buy a piece
out there they give traffic tickets

it has been going on a while

the women wear tight
and tighter pants
"I have a grip on my habit"
is what they say
when the gaze they court
reaches its destination
at long last

bad girls with glasses

I know them.
They know me.
When we have
a few drinks
we see each other.

I knew what I wanted

but I didn't just go ahead
having my way
I let ambiguity reign
my object of desire fled
to the kitchen
the pet fled out the door
what I wanted
didn't change
but I was alone now

the diners

hunger turns me on
only I am easily satisfied
some people want more
I can't be everybody's meal
ticket or meal regretfully
I must not answer the phone
ring on beautiful cell
it's not me you're calling
it's the food in my pantry
I should have taken you out

sheep (patriotic poetry)

life sans sheep's unbearable,
my curly-haired friends in meadows
of quirky late-night mythos!
my tongue peregrinates
as I digress on the big map
as soon as I take off the sheep
to lie down with a wolf!
guess what tastes like what!
I can choose among masks
but somehow the warm smell's
sweet underside's lulled by curls!
my country's sheep-fucking!
the love of a young sheep
for a boy barely above lamb age.
long ago sheep told bishops
where to get off & word got around:
tough sheep!
barely above lamb age when I met
her coat. the sheep police never sleep.
ms. pan the great sheep watcher should
know & does. it's a furry tear hangs
sweet like grass from many of these
sorrows, these sheep that have gotten
scads too much press from myth.

rory

huey long's grandson
lives in Boulder
his mother in her dotage
he is a visionary
who will with the help
of thermal energy derived
from pluto save the world
and cause his grandfather
"to turn over in his grave"
just another twist in a long
and colorful career

two

LU LI & WENG LI

preface

Lu Li and Weng Li lived in China in the Mongol Century (1279–1368). Lu Li was a courtesan at the imperial court, Weng Li was a warrior. They were either brother and sister or lovers or, perhaps, both. They wrote poems for each other without any certainty that the other would ever read them. All we know about them comes from their poems. Their first appearance in English was in *Exquisite Corpse: a Journal of Life & Letters,* where they were introduced in this way: "After the manuscript, carefully bound together as if someone were preparing it for publication, was found in 1989, two more years passed before a modern Chinese translation by Wang Shih appeared. The first translation in the West was into Portuguese by Dr. Alberto S. Figueroa from the University of Lisbon. This superb translation by Len Darien is from both the Chinese and the Portuguese." After publication, there was a wave of interest in these late thirteenth-century poets, and translation into German and French followed. A Chinese scholar, unable to find the Chinese translation in China, questioned their authenticity. "These poets," he wrote, "are entirely too modern. They speak across the ages clearer than most of us speak across the room." But this is precisely what poetry, from whatever age, does. Nonetheless, a wave of scholarly skepticism followed the Beijing professor's article. Faced with this near-universal distraction, Len Darien, the translator, admitted that there was no Chinese version, and that, in fact, there was no Len Darien. Len Darien was a nom-de-plume for the editor of *Exquisite Corpse,* who was indeed writing his poems from across the room to his muse Laura, who helped give form to Lu Li's voice while Weng warred. Both Lu Li and Weng Li eventually took possession of Andrei Codrescu, who faithfully wrote down what they said. Lu Li and Weng Li are not a literary hoax. Granted, they arrived in English in an unconventional way, but they are here, regardless.

today we had games
in the purple chamber
two rows of ten little feet
made a bed
for the emperor
mine were the collar
around his neck

*

I saw some writing
in a stream
I couldn't read
what it said
it said Lu Li
Lu Li Lu Li
there is a gray hair
among your black ones
it said that
I couldn't read it

*

no one came for me today
all the windows were shuttered
the emperor's son lay ill
the bad wind from the north
brought news from the war
Weng is there
on his horse riding
against the wind

*

I did not feel like being dressed today
I sent away my maid
I made a hill of my clothes
in the middle of the floor
the wind rattled the shutters
all day
I am no one without my clothes
I could have stayed like that forever
In the evening a messenger came
I stepped into my clothes
and was Lu Li again

*

ten red beans
ten white beans
a black stone
ten times in a day
I move them
no one else
can play my game
the cook surprised me
one of them I said
will make a meal
for the whole palace
she smiled knowingly
her hair is white

*

the cobra in the jade pot
was our dinner
our appetites differ
in autumn
the vulgar tongue
tastes my egg
secretly

*

he had so much flesh
it took three days to unravel
his wide belt
he was the emperor's treasurer
the empire was in his belly
even the moon did not rise
that night

*

it is always dark
in the winter
it is always winter
in the palace chamber
once the sky
was my window

*

the sweet-smelling one
left at dawn
a rainy day
he is going to translate
indian poetry
for our emperor
whose mind is far away from war
my beloved Weng Li
makes war far away

*

my friend's jade comb
looks better in my hair
the man who gave it to her
sleeps better on my pillow

*

I lie down
for a moment
clouds pass
summer is beginning
I think I will visit
my parents
in the country

*

an egg yolk in the pan
the sun in the sky
a goldfish in the pond
the gods made many round things
to make Lu Li laugh

*

magical ducks lay gold eggs
in places no one can find them
I find them
I paint them black
like swans' eggs
I do not want my neighbors
to know I'm rich

*

in the tree by my window
birds often lay each others' eggs
in each others' nests
I sometimes leave pretty underthings
in strange houses

*

the man a woman bathes
becomes her egg
the eyes of men
are hen's eggs
when they look at my breasts
they hatch fantasies

*

71

the rice wine was sweet last night
today I do not dare to open my mouth
for fear a foul wind
made out of words I carelessly spoke
will blow out of it
they are still laughing at the palace

*

for her services
the emperor gave his favorite
a silk farm
now she listens to the silkworms
spin the robes of the new favorites
in each one she hides an eyelash
when they wake another hair
has turned white on their heads
the new favorites age lash by lash
their bodies a field for her caterpillars
soaking up the moonlight of her loneliness

*

Lu Li's almonds
the paper sack
at my door said
it was still there
when I came back
a week later
from the country
no one dares eat
Lu Li's almonds
when she is not in

*

a loud voice
has no need of drums
a soft one
whispering to a pink ear
needs no flutes
what I have to say
is not all there is

*

puppets cannot be taller
than the emperor's bedchamber
a crier announced today
puppeteers cannot make people
laugh louder than the gongs
announcing the arrival
of the emperor's crier
the actors sawed off
the legs of their puppets
everyone laughed quietly
they were listening for the gongs
the emperor an old woman said
is leaving the empire to his crier

*

caterpillars are in fashion
women use them to clean their ears
men put them in their noses
in the city now
people sprawl in their homes
full of hairy worms
all in the name of beauty

*

the emperor has a red monkey
he strokes it so much it is bald
his sleeve always holds seeds
for his singing birds
he can only sleep on the fur
of a bear he killed in his youth
he is like a woman who chews
red beetles all day
or like Lu Li who sits on her step
outside her room rubbing smooth
her pretty stones
the empire is built of empty gestures
somewhere Weng sheds blood for it
on hillsides bald as the emperor's monkey

*

today was rainy
the palace was shrouded
I lost my way to the bath
the women laughed
here comes Lu Li already wet
they played with me
a bursting cloud

*

74

I slapped little Chen
for braiding my hair too roughly
she is only twelve
her mind is already elsewhere
she thinks of her own hair
all day long she looks past me in the mirror
she is my mirror I was once like her
my lady slapped me too
we women descend through the ages
on a ladder of hair
each one looks up in the mirror
of the one above her

*

the captain of the guards
the chief notary and
the tax collector
for the whole empire
were beheaded today
everyone rejoiced
at the market the women
gave rice cakes free
everyone shouted
the emperor is just
the hard men are gone
let them rejoice this day
new men are coming
to work at dawn

weng li

the village henchman
poisoned the well
threw himself in it
for good measure
everyone else fled
we set fire to the empty sheds
we were thirsty for water
not for blood
that night I heard
laughter from the well
next day we rode far

*

the snow fell all night
when I stepped out of my tent
the beards of old men
had wrapped everything
wisdom has come to us I thought
I heard a white mound groan
and another grunt
and one farted loudly
the snow is kind
but wisdom is far away

*

the crows read my writing
in the snow
soldiers write in the snow
for crows
the crows take our messages
to the cities
to make the merchants tremble
they gather in fear behind their walls
soldiers are pissing just outside our walls
they say and tremble and wait

*

the barbarian sang before we killed him
he was too weak to work
but he had a melodious voice
his stories were about spirits
he was already home among them

*

it might as well be said
Hun and Sen live together
like man and wife
and they quarrel the same
today Hun cut the gold tassel
on Sen's saddle
he bawled so much the enemy
came to spy on us from the hill
they thought our prince died

*

on a lone tree in a clearing
autumn left an apple
it is wrinkled and stubborn
an old whore's behind
everyone wants to eat it
no one wants the others to see him
the emperor's best men
are afraid of an apple
the shame will make us kill
more people tomorrow

*

there was no one on the street to greet us
the houses were on fire
we torched them all
a stubborn old man
sat on an old tree stump
in front of his blazing pig sty
singing a song to himself
I tipped my lance to him
he did not see me

*

78

sometimes there are two of me
Weng on his horse with fire on his sword
and Weng who walks in monk's garb
alongside Weng on his horse
Weng the monk will be the one
to see me depart this world
we each live in our own weather
the horseman lives in the spring
the dark-hooded one who follows
lives in the heart of winter

*

peace was concluded
yesterday between my lord
and our enemies
but today we rode into battle
to fight for ourselves
I held high the head
of a soldier I killed
for his harness and shield

*

Lu Li my beloved
sits on a cloud of incense
pleasing the emperor's
translator
this news has clouded my mind
I hit my horse hard
he looked at me without understanding

*

the village headman presented our lord
with two jade lovers
we passed them from hand to hand
each man thought of his loved one
when the figures were returned
the jade was dark
so many lovers

*

tonight our cook
found only a small dog
the broth was thin
the star in the sky
some call The Dog
filled our empty bowls

*

treason was twice punished today
a horseman was halved by sword
his foot soldier was torn to pieces
tied to four horses
from the hills the enemy watched
today we meet in the field
my lord and I drank silently all night

*

some of my fellows believe
that a man and his horse
go to heaven together
but why ride there
when you are lighter
than sunlight
we will ride alongside
each other there
horse and men good friends

*

in the purse
I cut from around his neck
were three gold coins
bearing the script
of another empire
a lock of black hair
and a small flat stone
the hair was the same color
as Lu Li's hair
the stone was like the many stones
I skipped on the Yangtze river
when I was a boy
for a moment I thought
the strange soldier
was myself
he was not
he was dead

*

they tell a story
about a country
where no one could read
the monks there
are unafraid
no one can see
what he writes of them

*

the philosophers quarrel
about how the world was made
some say the stars made us
others say that the gods did
I take no part in their discussions
I watch a boy watch a girl
the grass whispers when they pass

*

seven times in one year
I have written Lu Li
not once did she answer
seven times she read
every letter
she knows them by heart

*

by the side of the road
to Nanking
a monk so fat
three boys had to hold him upright
the dust of my horse's hooves
made a cloud of them
what stories were they telling?

*

when I was a boy
in our village
there was a fountain
a demon lived in it
one time I saw him
he was eating a leaf
war is coming
my father said
I am that demon

*

my fellow soldiers
have their way
with frightened girls
in burning villages
I do not play their games
I think of Lu Li

*

I have served under seven lords
some were generous with their gold
I like my horse best of all
we have ridden so far from home
he sometimes looks at me
I know that he remembers

*

I have no use
for the village I conquered
for my lord
the big house in the middle
of the town
looks at me
through the eyes of a young girl

*

when I am killed
my fellow soldiers
will find my poetry
under my saddle
they will laugh
they will say
all this time
we thought he was like us

*

I have killed another boy
flying the pennant of my enemy
I think about Lu Li
in the far-off city
she would have liked him

*

my master thought poetry
was for clerks
I have been wearing armor
these many years
I think he was wrong

*

the smell of burning
villages
is not poetry
the smoke on the empty
autumn sky
writes something there
it is not poetry either

*

my head hurts
I have not been wounded
it is not the fighting
I will march against myself
when I am better

*

no pig to roast
nothing in our bellies
others came before us
left only stubble
the city we say
is over that mountain
meat comes steaming
on porcelain dishes
in the hands of silken maids
after much wine
they fold like clouds
over our hard skin

*

the emperor's tax collector
took everything
they say
they left us only the skin
on our backs
take it the villagers
beseech us
we do
because we are merciful
we take their lives too

*

we found a scribe
in the burning market
bent over his scrolls
he saw no smoke no fire
no men on horses
write our stories

86

we commanded him
leave nothing out
for many days
he wrote down
what we told him
he did not wonder
where everyone
in town had gone
they were lying dead
all about him
the stories we told
were of our great deeds
he did not wonder about them
he wrote and wrote

*

in the imperial city
there are many kinds of light
and many shades of dark
the sun there is one among many
the emperor's chariot burns
like another sun
for us there is only one sun
we level fields under it
burn cities to the ground
sweat streams on our backs
fire burnishes our weapons
the sun is always overhead
our sun is one not many

*

a tower
made of bricks
must be seen
with eyes of steel
this is how men
of war think
the tower
of words
I am making
should be seen
with velvet eyes
those are not the eyes
of anyone here
I have to look
in the night sky
for those eyes

*

where there were dragons
cities will spring up
the storyteller said
he was polished
a speaking walnut
we had killed
all the dragons
but only he could see
the cities
I listened to his stories
I did not care to see
those cities

*

our captain went
from tent to tent
handing every man
a pair of wings
it is not easy he said
to keep these soft
all night I heard the men
smoothing feathers
no one flew away

*

in the year of the burning
horse-shaped star
many people fled to caves
in fear of the heavens
not my mother and father
they lay in the grass
under the broken vase
that showered them with light
I was conceived then
so said the astrologer
many years before the wars

*

our archers can hit
drops of rain
push their arrows straight
through the wet curtain
rain death on those hidden
in the valleys
such skill comes about
after years of practice
they practice with tears

coda

the emperor's ears
are grown weary of the phone
they have heard many causes
he had no idea Lu Li
had a cause
Lu Li he always thought
just was
and would always be
now the telephone
and the television
have warped her mind
one with its ring
the other with its models
of how life should be
next thing you'll know
I'm not the emperor
and you're not Lu Li
now only asses would think
such a thing is better

three

often after a public event

a pretty girl curly black hair
framing literary ambition
or a shy tall boy black curly
hair burning with sympathy

will say something in a foreign
accent to me we are from bosnia
hungarians or jews my mother
was born near your city back then
it was in another country

now we are from here what should
we do with our accents

do like me I say
keep talking

every morning

before the law takes effect
the ex-dreamer
wipes out the lab
with a cup o' java
the turks the turks
they are the only hope
they and the books
about them by the greats
from former yugoslavia
who wait on the shelves
we are books the people
in us are savages now
take shelter the monk said
in the shadow of the pen
they are coming for your head
in minutes

brâncuși's fish

it is 1930
& fish bird and turtle
have taken the center stage
explaining Constantin
to the world:
left Romania like a turtle
with an apocryphal barrel
on my back full of student
works & arrived in Paris
the night a great party at Picabia's
stood still for a moment;
flew bird-like into the new century
of airplanes and transatlantic
commerce; the Americans
wanted to understand flight
they were born to it
they wanted to know its art
but above all I loved
the sonorous silence
of the dark bodies
of the women of the new century
who were not afraid to swim
in the dark with me and come up
only now and then for a mouthful
of brandy and champagne
& who loved the stealth
of abstracting all that jumble
of objects that cluttered everything
in the cubists' pads & were made
worse by the surrealists

with their mania for measurements
& advertising; Mina Loy
who was struck by the kinesthetic
purity of my bronze bird
& Nancy Cunard whose fabled ships
were a fish fable, & Peggy Peggy,
of course Peggy & we swam before
& after my famous cabbage rolls
in the metaphysical whiteness
of the year 1930:
every year since & every decade
is turtle bird or fish
in 1989 my bird soared again
then labored the turtle on
its laborious climb
then comes again the fish.
things look up & away.
time, show us how you swim

how I got to america

for Kris, who really knows

I swam over a barbed wire fence.
There was a hair curtain & I scaled it.
Then we closed the window.
A rabbi hid me in his black skirt.
A priest lent me a cassock.
I dressed in a cow skin & munched near the border:
when the bull came I ran like hell.
They traded me for a couple of spies.
I got a passkey to the Western World.
I made a fake ceiling on the Bucharest-Vienna Express
& curled in there with two of my best friends
& a bar of chocolate. The train went to Athens
instead & we died.
I wrote a letter to the President of America
& he sent Jimmy Carter to get me
with a diplomatic pouch just big enough
if I curled up real tight.
There was a little war in the southern Carpathians
and some of us were catapulted into Yugoslavia.
I married an extremely rich traveler
looking for her roots in my neighborhood.
At about 10 P.M. on January, 1965
I got inside the transistor radio and surfed
the Voice of America to Detroit.
I wrapped my hand around the handle
of my broom and said the magic words:
take me to the highs, save me from the lows!
But how I really got to America
only Kris knows.

the revolution and the poet

bucharest january 1 1990

The poet needs revolution every decade
like the wounded need transfusions.
There is still blood on the snow in Bucharest.
The people with flags unfurled atop tanks
strike the perfect revolutionary poses
the tableaux vivants of years of Marxist
schooling. The French fall in love with them.
This is the snow sprung live from every
painting between 1846–1965 and sculpture, too:
the bronze train atop of which Lenin arrives
at the Finland station
where two lovers have found a dark place to love in.
Only now Lenin is down and the lovers are on top.
This is the new decade in Bucharest, snowy New Year
by the blazing candles of the martyrs' shrine
drunk with the millennium
schooling complete at last

eliade: a poem

for mircea eliade, who died
just before the romanian revolution

Eliade the tree grew
from my childhood
into my adolescence
to become Eliade the poem
I write in the branches
of my middle age.
I am part of the poem
that was Eliade.
I was born in the country
of Eliade. I left when
I was still a young man,
set out for a country
called Eliade.
Its other name was Chicago.
The truck driver who picked up
the young boy hitchhiking
at the edge of America in 1966
had never heard of Eliade
but the boy told him
that there were two worlds
inside this one and two kinds
of time the sacred
and the profane, that 1966
was also 1946 the year of his birth,
and the fact that he was only
nineteen years old didn't mean that
he was not also a baby
just being born

on his way to Chicago-Eliade
the two-in-one town.
When they arrived
in the town of Eliade-Chicago
the truck driver was
half-convinced they exchanged phone
numbers by the phone booth
where minutes later the boy called
the man whose name the city bore
in his mind.
There were small boats on Lake
Eliade that day
and a girl who worked in a gas
station kissed the boy on the lips
shortly after that phone call was made
and that kiss too became Eliade.
It is said of Eliade as of other great men
that he changed the world
but he knew that the world
springs to life only
in the mind of a young boy
calling his hero from
a telephone booth under the El
soon to be kissed by a girl.
Claude the Algerian burglar at the Y
showed the boy how to make money:
wait in this car he said
outside this big house while I
the Algerian burglar bring
silver and televisions from
inside. When he sold them
later that day he gave the boy
fifty dollars that immediately
became Eliade because he used

that money to stay ten more days
in the city of Eliade.
Eliade asked the boy
big serious questions
that were little butterflies
over the salad lobster and wine
they had at Club Eliade
and nothing mattered more
not books not speeches not honors
though the wine and food
were somewhat sophisticated
for his young palate.
Later he staggered drunk by Lake Eliade
and was told by a policeman to go home.
I have just had the boy told
the policeman the only conversation
worth having and I do not blush
and right then he didn't
to think of the inanities
I have uttered into his great ear!
Gods judge not and are always
fully there for little boys everywhere!
In the moonlight of the lakefront
the policeman was only half-convinced
but then he was half policeman and half
minotaur he was Eliade.
Next day the girl from the gas station
kissed him again and the boy
held her young breast in his hand
and knew beyond the shadows of doubt
(which that year were numerous and strong)
that the sacred had blown over them
and they were holy.
The kiss became gold

it had a little body with wings
called Eliade shaped like a breast.
In time it has grown brighter.
Over towns called Eliade
over forbidden forests
flew Eliade's soul
going home to the country
where he was born
followed by a kiss.

Later he learned the truth.
Eliade had been a bad boy
in a bad century
whose ideas killed many boys
and might have killed him too
the Jewish worshipper of Eliade
if Eliade and his boys had
had their boy-killing ways.

the failed encounter

in memoriam gellu naum

about when the red blade broke
and the Intercontinental Hotel lights went out
and the phone was vomiting a stew of voices
not yet used to speaking freely
I listened in the uncertain season:
"If you visit me Codrescu, come now."
It was in mid-January 1990
in Bucharest & I had been sent by Jim Brook
with a sheaf of new Naum traductions
and a bouquet of good wishes
from San Francisco to hand to the maestro.
"You can't go now or tomorrow!"
shouted my producer "the satellite
only goes overhead twice a day!"
"ok, but a Gellu Naum only once a century!"
& I was ready to defy the satellite
but then it snowed & two immense days
rolled by made from rumors and gunshots
not yet sorted out & I crowded in with the herd
of the world press spouting uncertain stories
into the satellite going like a sheep overhead
and Gellu Naum was mad at me
because I hadn't responded to his appeal
I failed to hear his magical stories
which were released into the wind of Now
while the idiot tales streamed down
from satellites into unread archives

the american dream

guy on TV
tells Katie Couric
he'll name his
three-month-old
after any company
willing to buy
them a house
his last name is Black
Crack Black?
Marlboro Black?
asks Katie
IBM Black?
Xerox Black?
She goes on
he protests
we will be very
very careful
but we have
to have the American
Dream don't we

What company
Laura asks will
risk the publicity?
It's worth less
than a sandwich-man
I say but I can
already see
that little Black
is the first of an army

of genetically engineered
logo kids
who when asked
what's it like to look
like McDonald's arches
will say
In the Beginning
Was Black

babies and the two

people call me
for babies

I don't have babies

they will stop
at nothing
these good
grown-up people
who will scale the facade
of any hotel
for the babies inside
the inside babies

their eyes look on
Tchelitchev
in the baby forest

where they come from
these babies

one fills my life with silence
one fills my life with noise
both empty me

I mix their noise and silence
and come up rarely full
inside one or the other

but for the fugitive
light I'd be solvent

in jerusalem on my 48th birthday

My mustache is all that remains of Stalin.
At the tomb of Jesus the miracles surround us.
Sister Rodica knows every single one of them.
The stone of Golgotha is cracked under us.
The blood of the Crucified washed the skull of Adam.
The candles of believers at Easter light from the Light.
The Light hovers before it bursts into flames.
In that hovering the sick are healed.
Not one but many icons cry and ooze myrrh.
Especially the Mother of God whose Doloroso Mementos
fill Jerusalem with womanly lament.
Endlessly the stones crack when God and His are hurt.
And the Wailing Wall waits for us and it heats us up
in the rain. We put our wet heads against it
and against all the soggy paper prayers in it.
A young rabbi reads a prayer for health. Hand him
twenty shekels. Across the wall on a ridge a solid
mass of black-clad faithful stands under a banner
welcoming the Messiah. A donkey laden
with gasoline cans descends to the Via Dolorosa.
Two horses have broken free & are running into traffic.
The Mount of Olives' olive trees look scrawny.
Scrawny they look in the Garden of Gethsemane!
And the young Arabs look at us with burning eyes.
And young Israelis with machine guns measure everyone.
The spot where the Mother of God fainted.
The house of the Last Supper.
The church over the spot where Simon Peter heard the rooster crow.
The tombs of the patriarchs.
The lion of David over the Damascus Gate.

The son of David Absalom in his grave.
The kings and the prophets of Israel in their graves.
The Golden Gate built by the Turks to stop the endless
comings of too many Messiahs.
City of Messiahs on my birthday.
From grave to grave in Israel.
My father's. The million and a half
children's flickering candle-lit souls in an infinity
of mirrors at Vad Yashem, Benny Hendel's voice
reading out some of them.
The tomb of Jesus.
The Wailing Wall.
Wall to wall graves, O Jerusalem.
The grave of old worlds, new worlds, future worlds.
Grave waiting for graves.
This is where I celebrate my birth 48 years ago,
everything either beginning in 1946 or 1948.
The German Transylvanian Hospice St. Charles
next to the walled-in Templars' Cemetery.
Knots of forty-sixes and forty-eights.
Miri once saw an enormous coffin go in the gate.
Full of the Templars' treasure, including the Holy Grail.
The Romanian Church at 46 Shiftei Israel.
And all around, Israel, a country of children
milling about the streets while the elder minority
eats cakes and debates the world around coffee tables
but mainly debates the Jews because to Jews
the most fascinating thing in the world is Jews.
"Can you believe a whole country full of Jews?" asks Benny.
It was the letters that got me, I say, the Hebrew letters
that always, for me, were a bit mysterious and forbidden.
And we remember the Haifa oranges of our Romanian childhood,
mysterious globes of gold wrapped in crinkly tissue,
black Jewish letters burning on it like midnight fires

in the waning late hours of Stalinism.
And in this late age of computers the Jews await the Messiah
and Christians are ready for the End Times and the Second Coming
and writers lament the end of the book
and the Dead Sea scrolls say many circular things
in the Torah-like scroll at the Israel Museum,
an apple core at the center of Jewish insecurity.
The bazaar throbs with spices and cassette tapes.
The muezzin calls from his tower. The beating of the clapper
against the bell is the sound of nails driven into our Savior.
Thank you, Sister Rodica. And you know what else,
Paradise was closed to men until the Ascension of Christ.
And then it opened and now all men and women can go in,
if they do the right thing, have faith, kiss the stones,
buy holy oil, rub it on the afflicted parts, and pray
for tolerance, as soldiers go by with young voices and big machine guns.

the vision & prophecy plaza

vision not 20/20

    but then
      as the good doctor said

the only eyes that cannot
    be donated
are the ones that stay open—

    do crows donate their eyes?

I the recipient of these
    eyes know my donor
to have been a crow—

when I close them
I see carrion
    I peck out its eyes—

and my friend the good doctor
      Mark Lieberman
          said, playing Space Invaders,
      "Oops! There goes another eyeball!"

but one out of thirty isn't bad—

laser surgery is a new field
for poets—

Homer, Milton, Borges
might have all been seeing
what times we live in
instead of being seers

of times that came and come.

the hidden jews

are sometimes one
sometimes they hide
in groups

faux maranos in new mexico
go to church then have
underground passover
in the mountains of morocco
a village of jews farms
and observes since spain

eastern european communist
party founders with changed names
are jews they did what they could
for jews but when they couldn't
they let the jews go
to their deaths the international
brotherhood of workers
being what it was
stalin hated jews
his murderer-in-chief beria
was a jew
they'll hate him not me
stalin thought so did
all the stalins in history
kings and popes let the jews
handle the money we need
if the people scream for blood
they'll go for the jews

the führer of new york nazis
was a jew the new york times
run by jews exposed him
he killed himself next day

how deep jews hide
and with whom
is my new interest
the not-so-hidden jew in me
is asking for an inquest

today

today I gambled away
three hundred and fifty
dollars enough to feed
three cuban families
for three months ditto
romanians or zaireans
what kind of idiot
does that & what kind
of idiot smokes & drinks
after all he knows about
it & mr. blake must have
been mistaken when he said
in lewis macadams' river book
"your friends on earth are
your enemies in heaven"
my friends in heaven
are still my friends
it's why I can keep doing
all this stupid shit
and still they care for me
dostoyevski said it best
it's a sickness and he was
sick & I the idiot
will try to be better

our gang

is it nice
to throw out the window
a man in whose house
you had sex
& in whom you once
invested a sentimental bundle?
was the question I asked when Leigh
wearing a black angora sweater
proudly announced that she had
just lectured to Oschner doctors
on the subject of self-
mutilation from a post-
modern perspective
& in the process she had
thrown "Freud out the window"
to make room I suppose
for Lacan and Saussure
& I thought this most un-
grateful, nay, a form of self-
mutilation given the place
Freud once held in her heart
& in her husband Richard's
fiction
& then Richard & Gwen & I had
an animated discussion about
formality & informality
European & American
& what public & private means
in history & in the consuming
classes created by advertising

& we concluded as we always do
that New Orleans where masking
is both serious & ironic is as usual
the best place & Gwen said some-
thing about self-discipline & I'm
not sure what she meant
because I think that just wearing
clothes takes a lot of self-
discipline as Jeffrey once
said much better
& then Anthony the Cypriot prince
who now lives in Boston
spoke to me about a vast non-
profit corporation dedicated
to world peace of which he was
the president & I congratulated
him on Cyprus' refusal to deploy
long-range missiles
& on behalf of Cyprus Anthony
thanked me sincerely
& then Daniel tripped by & whispered
in my ear: "And now
for something different!"
so I followed him into the men's room
where he proceeded to take out a tiny
tinfoil packet inside of which lay
a fine powder he proclaimed to be
heroin & he warned me & himself
of its dangers before plunging
the tip of his penknife in the powder
& holding it under my nose for me
to partake which I did
& when I returned the poets were
passing around the second corpse

of the night, this one on a theme
I suggested, namely, What Useful Things
Might Poets Do If They Were Not
Poets? and Dave & Vincent & Gwen
& Bill & Richard & Leigh & Daniel
& some others applied themselves
to the topic not at all but produced
nonetheless a gorgeous corpse full
of sexual & mystical imagery just
like the first one which I'd read out
loud nary an hour before
& then Michelle showed up
& announced that she had quit
the stripshow business & henceforth
she would no longer disrobe
for the plebes & when we pressed
her on the reason she said:
"A man not really bad looking
nor particularly drunk said to me
'I want to lick your ass!'"
& this is why you quit we asked
in amazement, the same
thought having occurred to us many
times & I said, "Maybe you should
have a talk with your ass! It's eating
you out of house & home!"
"Literally," burst Michelle, "I have
no money for rent & I have no job!"
& so a collection was taken on
the spot & Anthony the Cypriot
prince & I drew our ATM cards & got
enough cash to pay $250 out of $275
Michelle's rent & I said I hoped that
she wouldn't go to great lengths

for the remaining $25 but I think
that she might have because at the very
decent hour of one A.M. I left them all
in the bar while I went home to call
Laura who was pissed off at me like
always when I stay out past nine
& that was another night at Molly's
& another $200 out the window
like Freud & many other things
happened, like the pretty boy Michelle
knew who said he was working on
inventing a seven-breasted
seven-wingèd woman & I said
When you're done, give me her phone
number! and he said solemnly, OK.

writers

A writer friend of mine told me about
another writer an old man sleeping
with a young girl
in a story by Bernard Malamud
he wakes up in the middle of the night
she is giving him a blow job
it is exquisite it is still sleep
when it is done he opens his eyes
and asks her: What did you
do that for?
What did she do that for?
Ingrate old man! Old men everywhere,
should you be graced with such luck!
Indeed, indeed, above the sushi and the steam!
The kind of writer I am would be singing.
But I do understand the old man,
he's another kind of writer.
Bliss so amazing & so sudden
must have words to go with it,
he fears that
if she does not say something
he will die
because he is an old writer man
moved now to want a phrase
out of her mouth to take with him
the way she has taken
him out of himself.
I don't know if she said anything. My friend
didn't say. I never read the story. But clearly
there is a kind of writer
that gets old thinking this way.
Me, I'm just jealous.

the view from the baby seat

I got here in a thousand cars
humans without cars are sick
the Martian observers said
snails that lost their shells
eighty percent of the world is sick
but they are sick together
when a song makes them amorous or lonely
there is no place they can immediately go

I was once small and scared in my father's
black Packard in the 1950s
everyone was afraid of my father
because my father had a car
I was scared because there was
someone else in the car with us
sometimes there were five or ten
other people in the car with us

I see the invisible passengers
without eyes
without hands
without noses
without bodies
they ride inside our cars
the consummate passengers
the perfect invisible hitchhikers
you don't remember you stopped for
in nineteen-sixty-something
they've been in your car ever since
in all our cars ever since

every one of our cars the nicer
roomier snazzier cars riding up
through the decades like your income
or down it doesn't matter
they don't care
you gave them a ride and they will
be with you forever

what haven't they seen
what haven't they heard
what haven't they felt
what haven't they sniffed
what haven't they licked
everything

the blind guy with exaggeratedly sensitive skin
the deaf guy who sniffs everything
one guy is mostly tongue
one is the Perfect Bad Timing Passenger

some of these specialized pale beings
were picked up by your grandfather
or grandmother and then by your father and mother
in nineteen forty fifty sixty seventy or something
and rode in their cars until your folks died or got too old
to drive anymore and then they moved into your car
and are now in there every time you take the wheel

they are the Perfect Passengers
the Consummate Passengers

they've never spilled anything
they've never said anything
they've never interfered in your domestic squabbles

they said nothing when you were mean to your children
they didn't laugh when you cried
they didn't care when you farted or jerked off
they never questioned where you were going
they just rode along and fed on everything
with the one sense that made the most sense
which is why they live long very long
long enough to outlive you and move
into your children's and your grandchildren's cars
the Consummate Passengers

The blind man who passes his palms
over the velveteen
backseat of the family Impala
where G. poet and friend
drank in the car's exhalation
in his mother's garage
on a dark February day in Detroit Michigan
where they made the car and broke his father
a dark day in a season of suicides
the sky is a kind of dark mid-70s velveteen
somebody clever said after the funeral
one of those things said inside a car
that only can be said inside a car

The listening guy is not blind
all he does is listen
whatever he hears he hangs on the peg
of these inside-the-car phrases
I told you not to
I told you so
What is that supposed to mean
What's her/his name anyway
If I wasn't going to do this I would

This very minute
I didn't have anything to do with it
They made me do it
That's my business
If they don't shut up right now I'll have to do something
Go ahead and kill me
Do you want to get out right here Go ahead
Can you touch that a little?
Not on your life buster
Can't you see how pretty it is?
It's not real money
What are you looking at you'll get us killed
They are your children too

Years pass everything is recorded

And then there is the Timing Passenger
her job is getting there on time
but her passion is rearranging the incongruous
to produce synchronicity
she's the only one in the car the car likes working with
and loves almost as much as it loves the driver

The Timing Passenger has a nemesis
the Perfect Bad Timing Perfect Passenger
his name is Death and he's thin like cigarette smoke
he survives the folding of the backseat
he lives in-between the squeezed walls of the car
hitting a tree or another car
he's right there his thin shadow between
the bodies slammed like two bronze cymbals
giving up their spirits to the night sky
he's right there in the vw convertible
when the giant redwood looms out of the California night

and kills Jeff and Glenn
and he's in the car when their friends carry their ashes
to the ocean

Oh velour
Oh Chrysler Cordoba Corinthian leather
Oh Japanese limo with swimming pool
Oh Letterman aftermath limo!
This Limo Guy sure knows how to have fun!

I introduce him to distract you from the sadness
of all the Invisible Passengers in your car
for me the best thing is getting out at the light
but I will always ride I will never get out at the light
I can no longer live in pedestrian countries
I am permanently strapped in the baby seat
with all these people around me
Mom and Dad can't see them
maybe they saw them once when they made me in the backseat

The future is a series of better and better furnished wombs
eventually we will not need to leave our cars at all
we will be in paradise and we will be one with glass and chrome and nauga
Look the Martians will say They have cured themselves

two desert monks encounter the
christ of happiness, christina

After a century of wandering the desert
of Southern California near Pasadena
in Julian's beat-up Toyota
looking for certitudes and faith
we came upon a faux-Greek restaurant
in a half-built suburb, its freshly painted
neon grapes turned hopefully toward
the skeletal beginnings of a Sonic
and the square image of a coming Borders
and there we called for wine—
we had barely touched our retsina
when roaring from the empty night
a gold Mercedes braked in the red sand
and out of it spilled a mop-headed waif
wrapped in a scarf who called herself Christina—
Gentlemen, gentlemen, she cried,
do you by any chance possess the time?
We possessed no such thing but offered
her our watches and the whole night
and day and whatever other time we had
(and we had plenty, trust me here!)
as she threw herself laughing on a chair
and emptied both our glasses with great skill—
though I had quit a cigarette I lit
on glimpsing her smoky petit point panties
as she crossed and uncrossed her jambes,
she made my monkishness impy and iffy pronto—
they were her cigarettes in fact
Winstons with a ripped top she had thrown

like a gauntlet on the table between us—
I have everything, Christina said,
a beautiful Mercedes at my command
a virile Serbian under me in bed,
as many orgasms as I care without breaking
the not-so-fragile vessel of my body,
a multitude that loves me to excess,
including people you just won't believe,
I'm happy without surcease, like a wave
ridden by a dreamer in a happy dream
and I make everyone happy too,
do I make you?
Oh, yes, we hastened to agree, you make us crave
all the forbidden things we want to have!
We are but monks for one more minute!
And yet, and yet, she cried,
I question and I question
this happiness without end!
Am I mad? Why don't
I have enemies?
Why am I not sad?
I love adventure!
I am always mad
for love for money
for philosophy,
but why no enemies?
why no resistance?
why no iron bed?
no crown of thorns?
From happiness I suffer—
Suffer—suffer—and
on top of all I'm French—and
still I'm happy!
What is wrong with me?

126

We looked
We smoked her cigarettes
We shrugged
We loved her questions
We loved her without questions, too
We had no idea
we finished the retsina
and we switched to ouzo
her great happiness enveloped us
in this barely-sketched suburban desert land
at this faux-Greek eatery in Pasadena—
How can you answer Christ
The Christ of Happiness Christina?
You are the Christ of Happiness, Christina!
we told her, as she roared away—
We are no longer lost in the desert!
Our souls have grown by a hair & an iota!
Yes, Father Julian and I are found!
When we got back in his beat-up Toyota
we only found a bit of her dust & then the sun
set over the desert outside of Pasadena
filling us with wonder, longing, and regret.
If you see this poem, divine Christina,
make us a sign with your Winston cigarette!

what some of them were wearing

Mary's Indian pants had pockets I put my hands in to guide her body for the pinball lesson, only the pockets had no bottoms so my hands ended up between her legs joined in prayer. Karen was on her day off from the hospital where she nursed and was shopping in a boutique on Grant Street for a dress when I saw her through the window, walked in, picked up a dress and said, This is for you, and I helped her try it on, and then we made love in the dressing room turned as much as possible toward what we hoped was a camera. I got picked up hitchhiking on Highway One to Sonoma by a woman in a miniskirt who said after we crossed the Golden Gate Bridge, Do you mind if I masturbate? and I said, Not at all, and I watched her do that almost to Petaluma on the outskirts of which she came, so I asked her if I could have a souvenir, if perhaps she might consider passing my bandanna between her legs and imbuing it with her moisture, and she screamed, What kind of pervert are you? Get out of my car right now! so I did, bandanna still around my sweat-beaded forehead. I kept looking at Karen's platform sandals while I was fucking her on the mattress on the floor of her Berkeley apartment when a roach crawled next to the heel of one of them so I picked it up while coming up on the thrust and lowered it on the bug on my way back in and Karen said, Not so hard! After I got coffee at the Hyatt restaurant in Indianapolis I reached in my pocket for my wallet and pulled out Jane's brassiere just as the middle-aged waitress with the tall coif was poised to pour more coffee into my cup, so I said, I traded my wallet for this? Erika was wearing only her red pumps when there was a knock at the hotel door so I opened it and let in a very pretty schoolteacher dressed in a business suit who wanted to know if I was ready for my speech at the Education Conference I was the keynoter for, and I said, Come in, I'm not quite ready yet, this is Erika, and they both shook hands without a trace of awkwardness. Henriette was sprawled on Dwight Kensington's white leather couch in the morning with one foot on a pile of her clothes and I was sleeping on the floor when the door opened and Dwight stood there with a young woman, both of them clad in mountaineering clothes with ropes and axes tied to their belts, and Henriette opened her eyes and said, Who the fuck is that? so I introduced Dwight, and Henriette stood up and shook hands with both of them and I shook hands with the woman, Dwight's cousin as it turned out. Morena climbed a short tree on a golf course near Rheinbeck, New York, and then hung upside down from a branch so that her plaid high-school dress rode up and I was staring at her crotch just barely covered by a black thong which I kissed immediately. Laura and I made love on the golf course and the cops shined their lights on us from the road so I put her panties in my pocket and the rest of our clothes on very quickly and then said good evening to the officers who asked to see I.D., which I showed them but not before pulling the panties from my pocket, but they pretended not to notice.

my favorite boat has a horn on its side

It's the vessel of Ulysses sailing in the Aegean night.
Rolling sidelong on a ruffian wave,
the most famous sailor of all time couldn't keep his feta sandwich down.
The fish weren't pleased with the hero's troubles,
So they charged Joyce James from Dublin with rewriting the tale.
He dotted all the carnivals with a capital Z.
He painted all the flowers with other flowers' hues.
And the argonauts landed and cried the fish were possessed
or why else would they sport human tits and tresses?
Today's tails messed with yesterday's verbs
And up came modern lit out of ancient . . .
Heresy and humors brewing! Alack! Ach! WOOF!
Penelope's lost dog was sailing on the roof!

the party was boring

the people there
belonged to an uncertain profession
when the host put on a dirty movie
everyone fled
although what they all had in common
was having watched too much television
in their american childhoods
perhaps it was my fault
I should have started a literary argument
and come to blows with the young ones
it wasn't worth the trouble
there were no beauties to fight for

new orleans art for wall street

I was the most hungover man in the world
when I first attempted to make this work
in praise of New Orleans
for the consumption of Wall Street
I was to put it mildly hungover
but by no means either the most hungover now
or the most hungover in the past
in fact one cannot compare the hangovers of today
with the epic hangovers of yesterday
that in their splendid massiveness rivaled
all the hangovers of the ancient world
from Babylon to Sodom
given such hangovers it's a wonder
a true wonder that this city rose from the swamp
and held up under tropical storms
only less violent than the guts of the lyric citizens
I humbly admit to having but a midget hangover
compared to those colossi
and when I say that I attempted to make a work
I mean only that I thought of making a work
without actually putting pen to paper until later
which is now
and when I say in praise of New Orleans
I must qualify that praise with the deep wariness
of one who has praised before & felt quite insincere
on account of it & suffered guilt
which is a form of hangover
therefore I have resolved never to praise
except accidentally when carried away by emotions
too great to deconstruct

for instance this thing last Mardi Gras
with the dancer and the nurse and Laura
and the gnostics & the brand-new manuscript
of my phenomenal new book with all the feathers
floating around and the whole street on X dancing
in front of Café Brasil
I hate crowds if you must know
but that was praiseworthy so here it is.
And when I say that I wrote this
for the consumption of Wall Street
I am fully aware that Wall Streeters consume
no poems no matter how titillating or praiseworthy
and that this whole exercise is art
which is to say something you'll forget
as soon as I say so & I say so
Pay up first

robert has a newton

that turns your handwriting
into poetic misunderstandings
for instance I became
Media Cooking
the women discuss
their menstruation grant
the Finnish poet on the VCR
is taking his last journey to hell
no one can accuse this age
for lack of either substance
or culture
it's just that there are
so many histories to be wrapped
while the chief activity
is cooking
haddock in ginger sauce
there is also a party
to go to in an hour
at the house of a novelist
innumerable cultures will take place there
no one will write them down

last night at the relief

benefit for bosnia
two bishops on my right
two professors on my left

the beef donated by marriott
cooked bosnia-style
by the unwilling chef
is gristle with cloves
overcooked stringbeans

archbishop hannan
blasts the world
the europeans especially
for doing nothing
the virgin of medjugorje
is on disputed land

the professor says
in the thirteenth century
the west lost kosovo
to the turks because
of excessive piety
men should not hide
in monasteries they should
break down doors

I say
there are no more bears
in sarajevo there are no more
bears in the world

after the gristle
and the bishops
a very old woman
asks for a ride
last night she says
at the fairmont
at a similar occasion
the food was much better

in her eighties now
a first grade teacher
she said first grade
is the most important

europe needs to go back
to first grade
damn the gristle
bring back the bears

wartime questions & answers in montréal

1.

we know that
coulianou loved you
and he loved borges
and you published
an article in your magazine
that said borges was
a fascist how could you
disgrace coulianou
like that? and the man's
white mane shakes &
there is insanity in his eyes
eyes I could swear I have seen
before on a train
taking an old romanian nazi
from canada to new york
on his way back to romania
to die in the year 1978 or 9
in the years of ceaușescu
and these are the same eyes
and rumor has it that coulianou
was killed by the romanian
secret police with help
from canadian nazis
and I get the creepy feeling
that this guy accusing me
of god knows what is
one of the killers

and what is your agenda
you square-jawed fuckoff

without a country
and what are you doing here
among the jews you failed
to finish off in 1941?
but the israeli security guard
already knows all that & he sees
to it that I get to the car safely
at the end of the evening

2.

you are not a real journalist
and you don't know the difference
between reporters journalists
and holy seekers after the truth
like chomsky and others who have
shown us the evils of the united
states and why we deserve to perish
in the fires of hell
what do you think about that?

young woman with bad haircut
most likely caused by bad razor
I think that you are a caricature
of your father the antiwar activist
who lives with his boyfriend now
in a trailer on the edge of town

3.

this library
and many others
are full to bursting
with other peoples'
stories perhaps we
americans are ignorant

of all these other
peoples' stories
people like arabs
and kirghiz and afghan
the timid young man
with the soft heart
whispers & I say

lovely stories indeed
especially the ones
where these other people
kill every other people
not like them & then sing
songs of great folkloric
beauty about the glory
of reveling in their guts
at the bloody feast just
about to be reenacted
I prefer such stories
interpreted by american
jewish girls in montréal
in their folk dancing class
but never in their place
of origin

4.
you have told us
says the dapper gay man
with the expensive sweater
that you censored yourself
from writing about
the homoerotic cult
around osama bin laden
and I want to know why

this is a very good subject
and it might make gay people
feel proud

sure he's a handsome guy
I tell him & all gay people
should feel very proud
that such a handsome guy
can get other guys to die for him
& will turn their women
into blind eggs locked up
in darkened tents
he's as handsome as che guevara
whose handsomeness inspired &
inspires t-shirts and blue jeans &
hats & tattoos &
did you know that che was furious
when the russians pulled their nukes
out of cuba because he wanted
to launch a first strike against
the united states? and how proud
would we have been then?

5.
don't you know the wrong
people were blamed for
the tragedy of the world
trade towers they blamed
the terrorists instead
of the architects
and engineers whose
designs & buildings
were at fault?

and to that there was
bemusement no answer

6.
I have read the foreign
press on the internet
& they don't see eye to eye
with our press
why does our press see
things in favor of our
government which instead
of declaring the attack just
a crime declared war when
nicaragua years ago after
having its harbors mined
declared no war and the united
states is bombing vieque
and I'm puerto rican?

and to that bundle
of questions there are
several answers none
of which I am prepared
to give I'm not even
the press

9/11

with Allen Ginsberg in mind

9/11, I can barely remember you, they've buried you in so
much hype!

9/11, I wept when you were first on television! I wept for New
York, for the dead, for all of us, for myself, for the world!

9/11, I was sure that the world had changed forever because bad
guys wanted America dead & hated us because we listen to
rock 'n' roll and wear no miniskirts on our naked faces!

9/11, I cheered when our warplanes ripped through the skies of
Afghanistan scorching the caves where our enemies bur-
rowed & I marveled at our precision-guided bombs trying
to ignore their occasionally murderous imprecision!

9/11, I sat mesmerized in front of Fox News and CNN as the gar-
goyled faces of the Cold War began crawling out of the
musty cellars of history and, eyes unaccustomed to light
blinking, began to spout the doctrines of Total War!

9/11, I started to feel sorry for you when retired generals, admi-
rals, spies, loonies, and fakes brushed off their swords and
rushed to your defense! So many double chins! So many
watering eyes! So many dentured grins and brush hair-
cuts! So many double-bottom suitcases clutched in so
many pimp-ringed hands! They even brought Ollie North
from felonious disgrace to stand up for you with his
Constitution-overthrowing boyish old looks!

9/11, I felt bad for you when the Lefties crowded you from the
other side with their guilt-filled jaws of "I told you so,"
and their eternal excuses for the wretched exotics of the
world whose suffering they experience in their marble-
topped kitchens between arguments about what wine to
serve with the wild rice! And I wept for you again when
soured professors who missed the collapse of commie

facism in 1989 descended on you like rabid wolverines led
by Noam Chomsky whose teethmarks are all over the
zero ground of American academia!

9/11, you saved the paranoids from self-cannibalism!

9/11, you were a boon to advertisers and publicists and flag-
manufacturers, and they sold you with cars and pizzas
and they drained you of your raw primal power even as
they pretended to grieve for you! Zero down payment
until Doomsday!

9/11, you were a godsend to poetasters who were out of the
gate lamenting and whining before your towers even
gave out!

9/11, your dead and your heroes are covered by thick layers of
ash & greed & the Republic owes you an apology

9/11, I close my eyes and recall you in all your gory glory & I
still hate those who did this to us and to our greatest city

9/11, I can barely remember you & I'm sorry

alternatives

are what you get
when your first choice
is unavailable

prose is what I set out
to write
but had to settle
for poetry

in my forties

in my twenties
I set out to write poetry
ended up writing prose

now the choice is the alternative
and vice versa

it keeps me young

poetry by andrei codrescu

Alien Candor: Selected Poems, 1970–1996
Black Sparrow Press, 1996

Belligerence
Coffee House Press, 1991

Comrade Past & Mister Present
Coffee House Press, 1986; second edition 1991

Selected Poems: 1970–1980
Sun Books, 1983

The History of the Growth of Heaven
Braziller, 1973

A Serious Morning
Capra Press, 1973

License to Carry a Gun
Big Table, 1970;
reprinted by Carnegie-Mellon University Press, 1998

acknowledgments

The author is grateful to the following publications and their editors for first seeing some of these in print: "Three Nearly New Poems," a limited edition art book designed by Dan Mayer (2001); *Dispatch,* edited by Christine Monhollen (2002); *MSNBC.com* and Jan Herman for commissioning and posting what became "in jerusalem on my 48th birthday," (2000), published in final form by Nat Hardy in *The New Delta Review* (2002); Naropa Institute and Lisa Birman for the broadside of "today I gambled," (2002); NPR's *All Things Considered* for "9/11 with Ginsberg in Mind," broadcast on 9/11, 2002; the Weisman Museum in Minneapolis for inspiring "The View from the Baby Seat," a poetic lecture on cars (2002); Black Sparrow Press for the poetry of Lu Li and Weng Li, reprinted from *Exquisite Corpse* in Volume One of the two-volume anthology, *Thus Spake the Corpse* (1999); Michael Tisserand of New Orleans's *Gambit Weekly,* Ed Sanders of *The Woodstock Journal,* Alice McFadden of *The Free Press,* and my translator Ioana Avadani and editor Mircea Vasilescu of *Dilema* (Bucharest), for allowing some of these poetic intruders to sneak into my newspaper column; Carmen Firan for translating into Romanian, and *România Literară* for publishing "Brâncuși's Fish," "in Jerusalem on my 48th birthday," and "as tears go by" (2002).